M000103537

Ordering Information:

Quantity sales. Special discounts are available on quantity purchases by corporations, associations, and others. For details, contact the publisher at the email address above.

S. Habersham Educational Services, Dublin, Georgia 31021

FOREWORD

Poverty in the Deep South has always been an issue. There exist great examples of individuals who worked hard and were motivated to make a better life for themselves and others, and they met success. Dr. Hayward Cordy is one of those individuals. While we have moved past the era of sharecropping in the deep south, very little remains to remind those of us who fall into a certain age range of those days. However, the needs of our students have changed very little when it comes to overcoming poverty.

We may travel through rural South Georgia and see the small tenant houses still standing side by side as a stark reminder of the hard labor that went into the "privilege" to live in one of those houses. Landowners would provide small tenant houses for those that worked and sharecropped on the farm. The houses were an important part of the package deal for the sharecroppers. They usually had large families and needed a roof over their heads. There was an expectation that all able-bodied family members help with the workload.

Dr. Cordy is greatly admired by students and teachers who have worked along and beside him to make life better for others. Students in both Jenkins and Johnson County Schools have honored him. Students honored him by dedicating the yearbook to him in both school districts. While working hard and being a hands-on dedicated school administrator he was not always appreciated enough to be given equal pay when compared to others in similar positions. While he knew, that was not right it never disrupted the quality of service he provided to students.

Dr. Cordy learned as a young child growing up in poverty about hard work, respect for others, and performing assigned duties to a high level of quality. He grew up on a farm in rural Johnson County, Georgia. While his father, a sharecropper, did not have the opportunity to attend school his constant message to his children was one of excellence, always do your best. His mother and grandmother served as sources of strength as he struggled with low self- esteem seeing himself as "damaged goods". Being a chronic stutterer, he was often shunned by other students. Educators realizing he had much to offer intellectually gave support to those areas where he found success. Singing was one of those areas where he found success and affirmation. While singing he found confidence, and for that time in a song, his chronic stuttering was asleep. Living in a household with seventeen other family members was a training ground for building a strong belief system. He saw firsthand, what it meant to bring in extended family into an already full house and treat them as part of the immediate family. He learned that the real measurement of a person's life is in what you do for others to affect them in a positive way. He also learned early that life was not always fair, but that he determined his own destiny.

It is no surprise that Dr. Cordy had great support from public school educators. He has spent his entire life giving to others including students regardless of their background, race, or abilities. He understands that students must be respected, valued, and given the opportunity to learn and be successful. He is a model for understanding that as an educator he must have a clarity of purpose and direction for himself and students.

You will enjoy reading this book and you will be inspired, as I am, by the story of a genuinely outstanding person who came to know his capabilities and didn't let the hurtful words or actions reflected in the insecurities of others define him. With great admiration and respect for Dr. Hayward Cordy

Allene Magill Ed. D

Executive Director

Professional Association of Georgia Educators

DEDICATION

To those who struggle with life challenges,

I was thinking of you when I wrote the story of my life, highlighting my many struggles, fears, and successes. When I began to write, I realized that I was writing for me. I had to capture facets of my life journey in order to fully realize and appreciate the favor that has been bestowed on me. When juxtaposing my life's beginning and my status, I have seen my life trajectory skyrocket. Yet, deep down inside a piece of the little boy who struggled to just fit in and never quite did remains. The remnant that remains, a sign of my many struggles is now a source of strength. Not quite fitting in prepared me for a life of standing out and being favored to accomplish many firsts and what others only dream of.

To my mother, Carrie Lee, who bore and helped mold me, your strength is remarkable. To my son, Joey and many children, who taught me the impact of unconditional love, you give me hope. To my grandsons, Enrique' and Malachi, who bring me great joy, I see only greatness in you. To Annie Kate, Marie, and Kenneth, you provide much-needed support. To the rest of my family, blood, church, and work, you challenge me to recognize what for me is natural, must be cultivated in others. To Allene Magill and the Professional Association of Georgia Educators, your compassion and desire to highlight poverty and develop solutions inspires me. To S.Habersham Educational Services, who provided support in editing and fine-tuning this work, excellence defines you. Most notably to God, the life that I have been given and paths that I have trod was your plan for me. I am grateful for the journey.

THIS PAGE INTENTIONALLY LEFT BLANK

Table of Contents

INTRODUCTION

I began to put my thoughts and feelings about my impoverished state into words at an early age. One of my first writings as a young child, was titled "The World through the Eyes of a Ghetto Child". Johnson County, Georgia was hardly what would be termed a *ghetto*. My exposure to the word ghetto was limited to what I read, heard in the music of that day, or saw on television. I was very familiar with poverty however, having experienced it firsthand. To me, being relegated to where I lived because of social and economic circumstanced, caused me to identify with ghetto living. This is my story.

CHAPTER 1

Football Friday Night

It is Football Friday Night in Wrightsville, Georgia. Lovett Stadium is packed with excited fans eagerly awaiting kickoff. The high school band is preparing for an exciting half-time show; the smell of hotdogs and popcorn blanket the air. Make no mistake about it, its Football Friday Night! Football Friday Night in Johnson County has brought out many from the community since the football team won their first State Class A Football Championship title in 1979 led by legendary running back Herschel Walker and Head Coach Gary Phillips and staff. Herschel Walker went on to represent the small community of Wrightsville, winning the 1982 Heisman Trophy at the University of Georgia and becoming a professional football player.

On this particular night, I walked to the front of the stadium to greet the visiting team. As the superintendent of schools, I would normally stand at the fence located in the far end zone of Hershel Walker Field located at Lovett Stadium.

The high school principal normally did the greeting of the visiting team. This, however, was a special night. The Johnson County Trojans were playing the Jenkins County Eagles. This was the first time that the football teams had met on the gridiron in several years. What made this night so special for me was that I started my educational career in Jenkins County. I spent nineteen years working there. I have many fond memories of my tenure there.

In 1983, I was hired as a special education teacher. I taught all subjects to high school special education students. Later, I taught Related Vocational Instruction (RVI), which involved me team learning with the high school vocational teachers. This was an ideal teaching assignment for me as I had originally majored in Industrial Arts Education and had taken most of the content courses before changing my major to elementary/special education. Team teaching with the high school vocational teachers exposed my students to vocational education content and exposed regular education students to my students and me. Regular education students often commented about wishing they were in my class. In addition to teaching, I served as the club sponsor for Fellowship of Christian Athletes, coached girl's track, and volunteered to work at all school events.

I operated my classroom as a family environment. I had clear and high expectations concerning achievement and behavior. I taught an engaging, skills-based, relevant curriculum designed to influence my students' academic, physical, social, emotional, and moral development. My goal was to prepare students for life as opposed to preparing students for a test. When teaching my students about installment loans and interest, I secured sales brochures for motorcycles and cars that they liked. After researching the cost of the motorcycle or car, I taught them how to compute simple interest and the amount of installment payments. While it was common when I was a high school student, teaching students personal finance had waned by the time I began teaching. I taught them that credit was obligating future income. I also placed most of the older students in a work-study program at local businesses and supervised them. At least one of the students that I placed at the hospital still works there.

I utilized a response cost behavior management system coupled with positive reinforcement. Students started each week with an equal number of points. Students lost points for behavioral infractions or lack of effort. Students were awarded goodies and game time based on the number of points that they had left at the end of the week. Students were rewarded based on their choice of behaviors and academic engagement during the week. My classroom experiences prepared me for my role as principal.

During the spring of 1987, I was offered the newly created position of assistant principal of the Jenkins County Elementary and Middle School Complex. In this capacity, I was to serve two principals working with students in grades 3-8. Several administrative changes had a profound effect on me while at Jenkins. In fact, one can say they altered my life trajectory. The initial change happened when Dr. James Lynn Batten, was hired as superintendent during the spring of 1987. The second change came when long-time primary school principal, Mr. Domingo Green, decided to retire at the beginning of the summer. The third and probably the most profound change came directly from Dr. Batten himself. After being on the job for a few days, Dr. Batten approached me; then offered me an opportunity to lead Jenkins County Primary School as Pre-K- 2nd grade principal.

As the 3:10 dismissal bell rang on the last day of school at Jenkins County High School in 1987, I, a 26-year-old teacher with no administrative experience, walked out of my role as classroom teacher into the role of school principal. Overnight, my responsibilities more than doubled. I went from being responsible for the instruction of approximately 80 students to being responsible for approximately 700 children and 70 staff members. My support staff was rail thin. I had no assistant principal. I had no counselor. My only school-level support came from the three *Title I* reading instructors who were also tasked with academic placement. While admittedly challenging, my first principal's position afforded me an excellent learning opportunity. I was able to learn the intricacies of school administration and supervision. I learned how to operate a school on a shoestring budget; a budget that provided for minimal staff. My Jenkins County Primary experience would later prove to be invaluable. Not only was this position necessary for subsequent job opportunities, but it also allowed me to fully understand and appreciate the challenges faced by early career administrators. Now that I provide professional development and mentoring opportunities, I can truly empathize with the plight of the early leader! 1987 was a year to remember for me. That year the students chose to dedicate the yearbook to me. Students chose **me**, even though most of them had never attended my class. Students appreciated and respected my presence; even in informal settings. This token of appreciation affirmed my belief in the importance of even social interactions with students.

1987 Dedication

The Senior Class selected Mr. Hayward Cordy for the Eagle 87 Dedication. Mr. Cordy is a conscientious teacher who is dedicated to helping the students at JCHS. He gives freely of his time and energy to work with young people to instill values

and meaning to their lives.

CHAPTER 2

Family

I quickly learned that working with adults was much like working with children. Teachers, like children, crave acceptance. They want affirmation as well as positive feedback. As I checked teacher lessons plans each week, I made sure that I read them carefully. I made an extra effort to provide each teacher with feedback, providing what we in education call "content specific positive growth statements." I did not realize at the time just how much of an impact my feedback had on the teachers until recent years. Recently, one of my former teachers retired. She had worked at the primary school for more than thirty years. As a friend helped her move her belongings out of her classroom, lesson plan books were discovered. These lesson plan books were from the years that I served as her principal. When asked if she finally wanted to throw the old lesson plan books away, she quickly replied "no." She further stated that she had kept the books because of how affirming my feedback had been to her as a teacher, as well as a person. She was not planning on parting with them now!

Part of sustaining a healthy family requires having rules and invoking consequences. As principal, it was my responsibility to review and enforce our "family" rules. In performing this task, I used some of the strategies that I formulated as a teacher. I would walk around the school and make sure that all of the teachers had the tools they needed in order to deliver quality instruction. Additionally, I created evaluation instruments to assess the strengths and weaknesses of my teachers. I felt it was my responsibility to create a superior instructional atmosphere; one that both students and teachers could thrive. An immense function of ensuring teacher effectiveness in the classroom was making sure that they had what they needed to teach. Every classroom was equipped with a television for instructional purposes. One day I received a tip that one of our family members (a teacher) would at times turn the TV away from educational programs to non-educational programs. I personally had not observed the teacher doing so; therefore, I needed additional proof.

Now it was my observational practice to walk the halls. I typically left my office and went left down the hall. This particular day I decided to change up my routine. Rather than taking the left corridor route, I exited out the front door of the building and re-entered through the side door on the opposite end of the building. As I re-entered the building, I made my way to the "supposedly offending" teacher's classroom. I entered her classroom and sure enough, the television was on a non-educational channel. Not to make a scene in front of the class, I spoke to the teacher and children as always and quietly left the room. That afternoon once everyone had vacated the building, I had to invoke a consequence. I took some tools and removed the television from the classroom. I placed it in my office closet. The television remained in my closet for two weeks. After two weeks, I reinstalled it. The teacher never asked what happened to her TV. To my knowledge, we never experienced this problem again.

The family atmosphere extended to my students as well. Each day I arrived at work before 7:00 am. Even though, we did not begin school until 8:00 am parents that worked would drop their children off as early as 7:00 am each morning. Our procedure was for the first arrivals to go to the auditorium and sit. I did morning duty in the auditorium every day until one of the teacher assistants arrived at 7:30 am. While the students were waiting for school to start, I would turn the TV on an educational channel for them to watch. When the noise level became too loud, I would simply touch my right-hand index finger to my right ear and my left-hand index finger to my lips. The noise level would immediately drop. I would perform this gesture while saying, "Open ears and closed mouths." I introduced my students to the concept of self-monitoring. I taught them how to self- monitor their behavior. The feedback and support were reaffirming and quickly revealed my bent toward great leadership.

During my tenure, I only received one parental complaint. The complaint was from a parent once I instituted *Awards Day*. On *Awards Day*, we recognized the top and most improved student in each classroom. Students were awarded in each content area as well as in conduct. The concerned parent, after having gone to see the superintendent was directed to come and talk to me. The parent's bother was that not all students were recognized. Further, the mother complained that to award and recognize some students for academic and behavioral excellence and progress would stigmatize and negatively influence the self-esteem of the students who did not receive an award. The parent's suggestion was one with which I clearly understood. The parent suggested that I give every child an award. Having dealt with self-esteem issues most of my life; I empathized and readily understood the parent's concern and reasoning. I explained that my intent was to encourage all students to perform their best. I acknowledged that students have differing abilities, aptitudes, and talents. I stated that by seeing a classmate receive recognition would actually inspire others to work harder in the hopes of being recognized later. I respectfully and lovingly stated, "At some point in life our children will be compared to some standard. We want to do all we can to affirm them and elevate their level of esteem but at some point in life they will be judged by their performance and ability. To give every child an award minimizes and discourages individual student excellence." While the parent still had concerns, she respected my position and dropped the matter.

I based my opinion and beliefs on my own experiences growing up as a child of poverty. My father was born in abject poverty in 1929. He was a very smart and disciplined man. Unlike some of his first cousins who went to college and became teachers and school administrators, he dropped out of school in the first grade. My father dropped out of school out of necessity to support his family. As a young boy, he plowed mules for twenty-five cents a day. While he was not afforded the opportunity to receive an education, he was insistent that his children have the chance to do so. While my father could not read or write, he could do simple math in his head more quickly than we could on paper as children. He also knew the letters of the alphabet. On report card day, my father would do roll call. He would look at each of our report cards. If one of us happened to have a grade less than an *A* on our report card, my father would ask in his deep, booming bass voice, "What's that

B doing there?" He would then say, "You better pull it up next time." My father understood that his children were all different with varying talents and abilities. His message was that he expected each of us to do our best. If I was an *A* student, a *B* did not suffice. My father's constant message was that he did not have the opportunity to receive and education, but we did. We were expected to take full advantage of the opportunity. His message was not one of perfection but a message of always doing our best. His message was a message of excellence! This is the message, my father's message to me, which I conveyed to my students and teachers daily through word and through action. My message was that <u>each</u> of them had inherent value and worth and was worthy of respect. I further stated that respect beyond that which was inherent at birth was earned. I taught that exhibiting respect for oneself, good work habits, having a positive attitude, supporting others, and being a person of integrity earned a person a deeper level of respect. This has continued to be my central message as a leader.

CHAPTER 3

Transecents

After serving as primary school principal for three years, I was promoted to the position of Principal of Jenkins County Middle School. I student taught at William James Middle School in Statesboro, Ga. While there, I learned that middle school students, transecents, were and continue to be my favorite age group to work. I readily identified with transecents, those in the middle, struggling to find their way as they went through developmental changes and through life. While they were unpredictable and their mood and behavior was apt to change from minute to minute, their pliability in being able to be molded was so refreshing. Middle school proved to be my most rewarding years as a principal and I continued to promote the atmosphere of family. Apparently, students appreciated my efforts as I received the school yearbook dedication every year that I served as middle school principal; this honor was shared with a teacher on two of those occasions.

My primary school catchphrase, open ears and closed mouths was replaced with "give me the noise!" When I said this in the hallways or cafeteria, the noise level dropped immediately. Several years after serving as middle school principal, one student in particular affirmed that my message of excellence and accountability which my father taught me and which I modeled was being heard. One day the mother of a former middle school student who was now in high school called me to tell me that her son had something that he wanted to give me. I stopped by the house to visit with the parent and the student. He had made a wooden picture frame in his Industrial Arts/Technology class and had placed a tribute to me in the frame. Portions of what he wrote stood out and I have used this writing to teach others about the importance of establishing healthy relationships with children if we want to affect their lives. His taking the time to make the frame, cut the glass, write down his feelings, and somehow get the paper laminated had a profound effect on me. Some of his thoughts expressed verbatim were:

"I remember the time when you saw me in the hall one day when Mrs. _____ put me out of the class. You asked me about my grade and conduct. You looked at my grades and told me how important it is to get a good education. You said that working hard early in life would help because almost every job out there requires a high school education. Out of all we've been through, I still remember that father figure that you always gave me. I always looked up to you because I don't have my father around me all the time. I hope you understand that you gave me the will to be respectful and responsible. You remembered that I had a little brother and sister to look after. You reminded me that my mom needs me. Thank you for those encouraging words, and thanks for being there when I needed you most."

The student's stating that I gave him the will to be respectful and responsible brought me to tears as I read the writing.

I continue to believe that we must teach to the souls of children, especially children of poverty. By the soul I mean a student's thoughts, will, and emotions. Until we impact these areas of a child's affective domain, we will not see sustained academic and behavioral progress. When we, as educators, positively influence the souls of children, their view of themselves, their level of self-efficacy, and hope for a brighter future will change. This does not necessitate our having to spend large segments of time, which is in short supply. Teaching to the souls of children does require that our interactions with children be relational and personalized. In the case of the young man that wrote me to thank me, my interactions were both relational and personal. Upon seeing him in the hallway, I did not berate him or tell him to come to my office for further discipline. Instead, I called him by name while letting him know that I knew that he had an older brother as well as a younger brother and sister who would model themselves after him. I demonstrated that I valued him by my caring enough to know his name and family situation. I also used this as an opportunity to teach him that he was responsible for his behavior, attitude, and future and that they were all subject to change. This exchange was a three-minute investment of my time that affected a student for eternity.

After three years as middle school principal in the old Burgess Landrum school building, which was shared with an elementary school, a new middle school was completed on the campus of Jenkins County High School. With the resignation of the then high school principal, I became principal of both the Jenkins County Middle School and Jenkins County High School during the spring of 1993. At the board meeting where I agreed to accept the position, I was taken aback when one of the board members who had always been supportive of my performance as an administrator, objected to my being paid more than the current high school principal. Dr. Batten immediately reminded the board member that I was assuming responsibility for two schools for only $2000, more while saving the system more than $70,000. I felt that there were deeper issues beyond salary present in these exchanges, yet I remained silent. I decided that night that I would choose to do the quality job that I had always done and would serve as the principal of the middle/high school for only one year. I would not continue to serve past one year because I felt that my sacrifice was not universally appreciated. This cost savings measure proved productive yet a daunting task for me. As an administrator, I was known for having a personal touch and open door policy. This policy was being tested as I had an office on both campuses and had to travel back and forth between the two. The combined school principal approach allowed the system to increase its fund reserve and everyone was pleased with how well everything functioned. However, I was exhausted. Feeling that I had risen above the level that some expected and thought that I should rise, I set a goal of finding an administrative position outside of Jenkins County within two years. After one year of leading two separate schools and faculties, I asked to return to my position as middle school principal. My departure as high school principal was bittersweet as I realized that I had made a positive impact at the high school. I was quite honored to have the Jenkins County High School Class of 1994 dedicate the yearbook to me that year. This was an honor usually reserved for a teacher who had positively influenced the high school experiences of the majority of the senior class.

1994 Dedication

Endowed with the gifts of both a leader and an administrator, Mr. Cordy combines the vision and skill necessary to make our senior year a challenging and rewarding experience. We, the class of 1994, are blessed with a new principal who is fair, friendly, and genuinely interested in our welfare. With love and respect, we dedicate this annual to Mr. Hayward Cordy.

I left the Jenkins County School System at the end of the 1994-1995 school year after being offered a position at CSRA Regional Educational Service Agency in Dearing, Georgia. I served as Director of two distinctly different education programs that were operated separately in the same building. One was a program for severely emotionally, behavior disordered students in grades 1-12 and the other an alternative education program for disruptive students in grades 6-12. I was responsible for supervising approximately 175 students.

CHAPTER 4

The Match

The transition from administering general public education to dealing with students who were severely emotionally behavior disordered was difficult. I had not witnessed such behaviors. I could tell that the students felt damaged and in many cases had undergone serious emotional and physical abuse and neglect. While working with these pupils, I began to see a purpose for my growing up feeling damaged. Having experienced the damaged goods syndrome, I was able to empathize with my students who felt damaged while inspiring them to look beyond their damaged state and play an active role in determining their own destiny rather than being relegated to obscure, backseat living.

In my first staff meeting, I listened intently as the staff described what normal behavior was for our students. Stories of employees being physically attacked, spat upon, and verbally abused by students dominated the discussion. Having a background in special education, I understood those students and the issues that were inherent to the psychoeducational model. After everyone had finished talking, I asked if anyone had a match. Everyone looked surprised and waited for me to elaborate. I said to them, "I accept that what you describe is how these children are but if you believe that this is how they will always be, let's take a match and burn the place down right now and not waste the tax payer's dollars." My message to staff was simply this. I agree that we must unconditionally accept students as they are yet because we desire their better good, we must not leave them where we find them. We must meet them where they are. We must make them better by having been with us.

I was tested my first day with students. A new teacher in one of the upper elementary school classrooms called for me to come down to her classroom. This student mimicked me stuttering and looked at the teacher and asked, "Miss would he file charges if I hit him?" I leaned my head to the right in what I would call "Clint Eastwood style" and just looked him in the eyes to affirm for him that his comments did not evoke feelings of fear in me. I followed our school-wide behavioral plan in responding to this student's choice of behaviors. Had I shrunk back or shown any signs of fear, I would have been rendered ineffective. I learned as a teacher and principal that I set the tone for the year on the first day of school.

Children often use anger, aggression, and acting out behavior to control others or to push others away from them, thus avoiding them risking a continued pattern of rejection. We must teach children that it is not acceptable for them to hurt themselves or others. Through the affective domain, we can help students to feel and thus act more responsibly. We cannot actually teach children if we fear them or if they fear us. We must teach them to have respect for us through building positive relationships with them. Building positive relationships requires mutual respect, clearly established boundaries, and rewarding appropriate behavior while providing appropriate consequences for negative behavioral choices.

To students who lacked or who chose not to demonstrate self-control. I became *The Wall*. These students often acted out as a means of expressing their damaged state or as a means of control. In becoming their wall, I reminded them and daily demonstrated in actions that I cared for them as students and as individuals. I however reminded them that there were certain behaviors that were not acceptable. I let them know that I would respect them and that they would respect me. I let them know that as *The Wall*, what I expected from them today I would expect tomorrow and the day after.

After two years at CSRA Regional Educational Service Agency, I began to see much progress in the students. Student behavior improved. Behavior developed to the point that we were able to start a chorus. Having had a commercial driver's license since I was 18, I drove the borrowed school bus. Our choir sang at area nursing homes and other facilities. The performances were a source of pride for our teachers, students and the places where we performed. During our performances, we never had a student to act out or behave inappropriately. After one such performance, we treated the students to lunch at the *Golden Corral* Restaurant in Augusta, Georgia. Several restaurant patrons came to our table and complimented the students on their uniforms and on their behavior. As they inquired about where we were from and learned a little more about our students, they commented that our students behaved better and were more respectful than other children that they see in restaurants. The students smiled as they were complimented.

One of my greatest moments was when a student who had been at the school since Pre-kindergarten for violent and aggressive behavior improved to the point of being able to be dismissed from the program and begin his first regular school experience as a high school freshman! The staff warned me about this student when I became director as he repeatedly injured staff. I made a home visit soon after becoming director. The mother connected with me and told me that he was not any trouble at home and that I had her permission to raise him as if he was my own. I took her words to heart and provided him with unconditional love and acceptance coupled with individual accountability and respect. The mother's support and my unwillingness to accept her son's current behavior as a permanent condition nor way of life transformed the child's life. If we are to change the lives of children, it is imperative that school and family work together. The same message and expectations must be conveyed at home and at school if sustained progress is to be made. While an "us against them" attitude appears to be the rule of the day, collaboration is possible. <u>If we engage parents in a personal way and communicate progress and positive events, even if small, parents will more readily support the school</u>. If the first and only communication that a parent receives is when the child's behavior or academic progress is not what it needs to be, support from the home is unlikely. If we develop meaningful positive relationships with parents and caregivers, trust will develop and they will help hold their children accountable.

My message of unconditional acceptance, loving relationships, modeling appropriate behavior, accountability, and responsibility allowed us to move students who nobody wanted, nor had any hope for to a position of seeing themselves as being identified by their successes more than their disabilities and issues. I refused to leave them where they were.

Several years after leaving my position with CSRA RESA, I received an email from a former middle school student, who had been placed in one of the educational programs that I directed. He had since moved out of state and had become an accomplished musician. He had gotten married and had three sons. He and I still remain in touch from time to time. Most recently he completed his bachelors' degree in a health- related field and serves as director of the program. . One day I received a profound message from him. The message read *"You may not remember me, but I definitely remember you….you really encouraged me years ago. I was one of your students at____. Its been almost 9 years sense ive seen you doc!! Lol! There are sooooo many things id love to tell you doc that would take forever to type in an email…lol! But I just want to say that at that time in my life I was so depressed. I didn't feel like I had a friend in the world. I felt like no one cared about me or understood my pain. I didn't have an active male figure in my life…until I met Dr. Cordy. I know its been a while and a lot has transpired over the years, but I just wanted to say thank you. Thank you for your kind heart, thank you for showing that you really cared about me. I'll never forget the times when you would have to paddle me but what was so special about it was that fact that you'd always hug me after…Then you'd share your lunch with me!! You usually had chicken fingers and fires!! Lol!!…But because of that I knew you did it cause you truly cared about me …So anyway, I just had to look you up and tell you this. And no matter where I go or who I meet ill never forget the impact you had on my life. Thanks from the bottom of my heart. Much Love".*

CHAPTER 5

Overcoming Many Odds

In July 30, 2000, I began my tenure as Superintendent of Schools for the Jenkins County School System. The previous superintendent retired that spring leaving an opening. A search firm had been used in the selection process and I found out later that I had been the top candidate from the beginning of the selection process. Typically, the new superintendent begins his or her tenure on July 1st of the first year of their contract period. I later came to understand that the Board of Education for Jenkins County Schools was aware that I was the most qualified and best candidate for the position. Yet, they delayed making a final decision until mid-July due to concerns of feelings within the community, as I would be the first minority superintendent in the history of Jenkins County. When I became high school principal and at this time superintendent, I was not invited to be a member of Rotary Club as previous and future secondary school principals and superintendents were. It took the Rotary club six years to extend an invitation to me. This slight deeply bothered me. Not only did it affect me personally, I felt as though it affected the students as well. This lack of exposure limited my ability to brand my message to all segments of the community and get the support of the community. I felt rejected. However, I had no control of this situation. Having faced rejection before due to poverty and being a stutterer, I chose to focus on what I did have control over.

Once named, I found acceptance and support within most of the community and worked on building a spirit of family and excellence. My six-year tenure as superintendent was the most rewarding experience in my educational career. It was rewarding being able to see the progress of students whom I had served as their principal when they began school in kindergarten then transitioned to middle school and now stood before me as superintendent to declare them Jenkins County High School Graduates. I was fortunate to see my last class of kindergarten students when I served as principal walk across the stage and turn their tassel before I left Jenkins County. One student in particular stood out. He brought a handwritten letter over to my office during his senior year. I had been his primary school principal, middle school principal, and began my tenure as superintendent his senior year. He too had been a child of poverty and had been raised by a single but supportive parent. I saw that spark and love of learning in him and encouraged him continually. He thanked me in his letter for helping him and being his role model. He went on to graduate from both Morehouse College and Georgia Institute of Technology.

I left Jenkins County to return home to Johnson County, my birthplace during the summer of 2006. I began serving as the primary care giver for my then 79-year-old mother. I was also primary caregiver to my then 38-year-old niece who had Downs Syndrome. It was becoming increasingly harder to meet the needs of my mother and niece's needs even living only an hour's drive away. My mother falling face down onto the concrete in the winter of 2005 after going into the store was the deciding factor in my choosing to leave Jenkins County. Leaving Jenkins County and going back home to Johnson County was a very difficult and life changing decision. It meant leaving the house that I had designed and had built as well as my two grandsons that I loved dearly who lived only three miles away. It meant leaving a community of people that I had come to love. It meant leaving a system where I knew every family and family tie as well as most children by name; having done morning duty at the schools each and bus duty each afternoon. I felt as if I was leaving home to return home.

My appointment as the first Black person to serve as Superintendent of the Johnson County School System generated much publicity. This, I believe, was due in part to the perception among some in the area that Johnson County had continued to experience a racial divide among its citizens while other rural central Georgia towns had moved on. This perception, most likely grew out of national media attention drawn to the community due to highly publicized unrest that began during the tumultuous late 1970's and early 80's.

While my appointment had been somewhat of a novelty occurrence, to my knowledge, it was by no means highly controversial from a public perspective since I was a native son returning home. I recalled being asked by a reporter shortly after my appointment if I was surprised that the school board had appointed me due to my being Black. My response to him was that I believed that we had come to a point and time in history when people judged you by your character and work ethic more than on the color of one's skin. The subsequent article that followed began with the headline "Incoming Johnson County Superintendent Overcomes Many Odds." Among the many odds discussed was the fact that a native of Johnson County had overcome poverty and family illiteracy, being the twelfth child of thirteen children born to sharecroppers. The article also discussed my struggle with overcoming a chronic stuttering problem.

A conversation between two men in the hospital waiting room shortly after my being appointed superintendent left me with many questions. I had taken my elderly mother to an area hospital to have some tests run. I was sitting in the hospital waiting room thinking of so many things that I had to get done. Having spent several hours there already as my mother finished up a series of tests, I sat there with my glasses off in somewhat of a sleep-induced fog. A conversation coming from my left caught my attention, rather waking me out of my stupor. I looked up to see two men standing about twenty feet away from me conversing. One of the men appeared to be middle aged while the other man seemed to be eighty years old or older. After some talk about a previous local election, the conversation shifted to the topic of the inability to get enough workers today. A statement by the older man caused me to listen intently. He stated, *"You know it's hard to get anything done now days without good workers, especially when all you have is _____." The younger of the two men nodded in agreement. The older man continued with, " I'm a little upset with the school board, I really can't see that well, I see with a magnifying glass. But the gossip is at the restaurant, they tell me that the most prestigious position in the County, the superintendent, the school board has gone and hired them a _____." The younger man responded, " I was disappointed too."*

Their comments on race caused me to reflect on the headline, "Incoming Johnson County Superintendent Overcomes Many Odds." I began to ask myself many questions. 1) Have I actually overcome the seemingly insurmountable obstacles of poverty, low self-esteem and feelings of inadequacy associated with being a chronic stutterer only to be sidelined by race? 2) Do the thoughts of these two men reflect the majority opinion or the opinion of only a few? 3) Did I make a mistake by leaving Jenkins County, a place where I felt totally accepted and respected as person and a leader? 4) Did my having just complete a doctorate degree from a state research university mean nothing? 5) What more could I do to ensure that I was indeed judged solely on the content of my character by all? 6) Didn't my defying the odds and being a Black male with no police record or any other type of negative background factors matter. Questions, Questions abound. Should I have been hurt by the words spoken by the older man and affirmed by the younger man? Do most people still see color first? Is the color still the predominant factor by which we all judge each other? The answers to these questions rest in the hearts of each of us as individuals. I have resigned myself to the fact that I must maintain my long-standing approach to life. Having dealt with abject poverty, low self-esteem, being ostracized by others, and never quite fitting into the mold, I have learned to love and be comfortable with myself just the way that I was created. I chose that day to focus on the job at hand and do my best work. Whether the perceptions of these two men, of whom I both know, were isolated of prevalent, the problem was theirs and not mine. I learned years ago that when I begin to own others' problems, I take on their prescribed identity of me, their designated role for me in life, their negativity, and their shortsightedness. I chose to continue to believe that most people would respect me if I continue to be respectable, honest, and productive.

CHAPTER 6

CETA

The rattle of a diesel bus engine jolted me back to into the present. My thoughts returned to where I now stood, Lovett Stadium in Johnson County, Georgia. The team bus from Jenkins County entered Lovett Stadium. I walked over to greet the team and my former colleagues. I talked briefly to the coaches and some of my former students. The visiting team players and coaches then headed for the locker room. I continued to stand on the stadium bank, which stands between 15 and 20 feet above the field itself.

As I stood there on the bank, looking out on the field in the direction of the scoreboard, my mind flashed back to when I worked in the same stadium as a CETA student worker while in high school. President Richard M. Nixon signed CETA; the Comprehensive Employment and Training Act into law in 1973. President Jimmy Carter expanded the CETA

Program in the late 1970's in order to reduce unemployment
and spur economic growth. The portion of the expanded
CETA Program that I worked was designed to provide training
and employment for underprivileged youth. At one time, I
worked after school sweeping classrooms during the academic
year but worked primarily during the summer. I supervised a
group of high school students while washing school buses. I
also cut grass as well as did many other odd jobs during the
summer.

One day during the summer of 1978, the beginning of
my senior year in high school, I was busy cutting grass on the
football field using a push mower. It had rained recently and the
grass had grown quickly. The push mower shut down several
times as I cut through the tough grass. As I bent down to
restart the mower, I sensed that someone was watching me. I
looked up and noticed that someone was standing on the tall
bank looking out on the field at me. I immediately recognized
the person as being the long -time elected Superintendent of
Johnson County Schools. The superintendent was a shorter
man who always wore slacks and a blazer. A familiar fixture was
the cigar that always hung in his mouth. It was never lit but
always present.

From time to time, the superintendent would drive up
in the school's old blue AMC Rambler. He would stand
watching me cut grass from the bank. He would fold his arms
tightly across his waist with his cigar held tightly in the right
corner of his mouth. He would rock back and forth and smile
as he watched me cut the grass on the football field. I cranked
the mower again and resumed my long lanky stride and
advanced on the grass once again. I attacked the grass with
vigor and speed. The maintenance supervisor later told me that
the superintendent often remarked to him about how much he

enjoyed watching me work, often commenting, "those Cordy boys will burn a mower up, they really know how to work." I smiled and told him that I had been taught growing up that there were dignity and value in the work and to "always do your best and let your work speak for you."

As I looked out from the bank of Lovett Stadium that Football Friday Night, I was reminded of how far and from whence I had come. To my right sat fans from Jenkins County, the system where I began my teaching career and ended my tenure there as Superintendent of Schools. To my left sat the fans from Johnson County, my hometown, where I currently served as superintendent of schools and had grown up. Once again, my mind reflected on my past in Jenkins County and my past and present in Johnson County. I reflected on the many metamorphoses that my life had undertaken over the past 54 years. My life had been an arduous journey filled with much success and moments of consternation.

That fall night, I stood on the same bank in Lovett Stadium where the then Superintendent of Johnson County Schools stood watching me cut grass as a boy. For the first time in my life, I realized and reflected on the significance of my standing on that bank. Standing on the bank gave one a vantage point from which the entire stadium and all of the schools could be viewed with a quick glance in either direction. That night I stood looking out from the same vantage point from which my work had been previously observed, respected, and assessed many years ago. This same vantage point had become a vantage point from which I could now see, respect, and evaluate my work as the current Superintendent of the Johnson County School System.

As a child of poverty who had been crippled by a speech impediment, the vantage point from which I now stood was only an improbable dream. An improbable dream had become my reality. Being back home allowed me to recount some of the lived experiences that I had faced growing up as well as in my adult life. The challenges and memories of the impact of poverty and rejection dominated my thoughts. Most people who knew me outside of my hometown always assumed that I had come from a middle-class upbringing. They were always shocked to find that I had been reared in conditions of abject poverty and in a state of perceived constant rejection due to my being a chronic stutterer. None of them knew that during my developmental years that I saw myself as others saw me, "Damaged Goods."

CHAPTER 7

Damaged Goods

G rowing up in the small southern town of Wrightsville, Georgia, one of my fondest memories is that of going to town with mama and daddy on Saturdays. Being raised in the rural south, we did not see the town often, except when passing through on the school bus each day. Before daddy bought his first car, an old brown 1957 Chevrolet, I vividly remember him borrowing his boss's Ford pickup. We would ride to town on the old truck on Saturdays. Mama and Daddy sat in the cab; the children would sit on the back. We would take the wooden chairs that we sat in at home and place them in the bed of the truck and proudly ride into town. It was a balancing act to remain in a vertical and seated position as the chairs slid across the truck bed. The chairs would bounce with each turn and bump in the road. Despite the sometimes rough ride, we were always excited to go.

Mama and daddy shopped at a local "mom and pop" grocery store with the name emblazoned on a metal Sunbeam Bread sign. A Coke machine stood watch by the front door. Mama and daddy shopped the aisles for a few staples such as grits, rice, sugar, and flour. They would then head back to the meat counter where the owner, who also served as butcher, always stood behind the meat counter with a cigar and a smile.

The owner always saved boxes of reduced price meats and damaged can goods for daddy to buy. As a child, I can recall thinking how thoughtful it was of him to save the reduced price meat and damaged can goods for us. Mama and daddy could not have provided food for our eighteen-member household had it not been for the local grocer. Our family consisted of thirteen children, a cousin, Grandmother Carrie, great Aunt Minnie, and mama and daddy. The reduced price meat and damaged can goods provided necessary subsistence. We had a large garden and out of necessity grew the vegetables that we ate. We also raised pigs, goats, and chickens for food. Mama and daddy bought meat from the grocery store only when the meat supplied by our butchering three hogs each year began to run low.

In the back of my mind though, I can remember the funny feeling that I got when I saw other shoppers going down the aisles, filling their buggies with bright, shiny perfectly round cans and freshly cut meat. Poverty forced us to buy the damaged can goods and reduced price meat. The damaged goods that my parents bought served to remind me of the poverty that permeated my life.

Besides reminding me of my living in poverty, somehow, the damaged can goods and reduced priced meals mirrored my inner feelings about myself. The constant teasing and ridicule from others due to my being born a chronic stutterer often left me feeling like the damaged goods and reduced priced meat that we bought. I quickly discovered and was regularly reminded that I was not perfectly round like the cans purchased from the grocery store shelves. Unlike the rest of my family and classmates, I was imperfect. I became aware that I was perceived as being like the damaged cans that mama and daddy bought. I sensed that others ascribed a lesser value to me just as the store owner did to the damaged can goods and reduced price meat.

I recall being teased at school and at home on a regular basis. With nine boys in the home, we had our own ready-made basketball, baseball, and football team. We had a full court dirt basketball court in the backyard and often hosted pickup games for those living in our community as well as for those living in town that would walk or catch a ride to our house. While my brothers were excited when the other boys showed up for a quick pick up game, I dreaded it. I knew already and was actually relieved that I would not be chosen to play on a team. I stood around and watched alongside other fewer talented players cheering my team on. I loved sports and even though I had the size, build, and attitude necessary to be a great athlete, I lacked the coordination and motor skills necessary to be a good athlete. These pickup games and the accompanying disparaging comments such as "you are a big sorry joker" reminded me that I actually was damaged. I accepted the comments without reply as I felt deserving of them.

I was very uncoordinated and exhibited distinct deficits in fine and gross motor skill development from an early age. I attended Dock Kemp School until the schools integrated the year that I entered 4th grade. In first grade at Dock Kemp School, as a student in Ms. Evelyn Williams' class, I remember not being able to skip as we played outside at recess. She was aware of my deficits but made an extra effort to provide me with opportunities in which I could excel and always encouraged me. My 1st, 2nd, and 3rd-grade teachers, Ms.

Williams, Ms. Shirley Pierce, and Ms. Newman Brown
respectively focused on my strengths rather than my
weaknesses. I was chosen to sing all stanzas of We Three Kings
for our school Christmas play one year. I had never owned a
bathrobe and had to borrow one from the owner of the land on
which we lived. As is the case with stutters, I sang with perfect
pitch and enunciation, as stutters do not stutter when they are
singing.

        I became more uncoordinated at the onset of puberty.
It would be the beginning of my tenth grade year before my
coordination improved to the point that I finally felt "normal."
My intellectual development stood in stark contrast to my
motor skill development. Intellectually however I had always
excelled. I learned to read and write at an early age. This ability
proved to be quite useful as I grew up. One of my older
brothers recently recounted a childhood memory of my
precocious ability to read and write. Being the youngest of the
nine boys in the family, I often was allowed to follow my older
brothers around. I would observe and absorb every word said.
Later I would write down everything that my brothers said-
including the curse words. I would then give the paper to my
mother. My brothers would respond, "That little joker can
write, can't he." I credit my early emphasis on writing over
speaking as the reason that I continued to excel as a writer to
the extent of being recommended for and taking honors
English courses in my undergraduate program at Georgia
Southern.

        My early aptitude for academic success could not
drown out the voice of my deficits. The constant message was
that I was weak, imperfect, damaged. I was mimicked and
teased about being a stutterer on a daily basis. I never cried or
lashed out at my tormentors. Unlike the youth who experience

rejection today, the idea today of "going postal" or retaliating with violence was not in my repertoire. As a child of poverty growing up, I was taught that respect begins with oneself. That legitimate self-esteem and self-respect were not so fragile that an unkind word would catapult one into a fit of revengeful rage. I was taught that I was worthy of respect simply because I was a human being. I was taught that I earned legitimate respect by being respectful and through honest and hard work. When others made disparaging comments, I responded with a look of indifference or with a smile as if to indicate that the comment was not worthy of a response. Yet, deep inside, each occurrence of teasing further solidified in my mind that I was damaged.

I was always a gifted student and was somehow able to compartmentalize my ineptness in regard to motor skill deficits. This included playing sports. I did not allow it to bleed over and affect my self-perception concerning my intellectual capacity and classroom performance. This was not true however if my classroom performance required me to do an oral presentation or anything beyond answering a question. If I had to do any type of oral presentation, I would begin talking and my rate of speech would quickly go from normal to rapid. This can be an automatic response in stutterers as it allows the stutterer to finish saying what needs to be said before the onset of a pattern of stuttering begins. Most of the time, I ended up speeding through the presentation and then sitting down, feeling embarrassed. My classmates and teachers became accustomed to my speaking rapidly. I was bothered by it even though I could not control it. I recall one of my social studies teachers commenting after I had made an oral presentation, "Hayward will be alright once he realizes that nobody is going to bite him." How I wished that it had been as simple as my teacher suggested had. Although feeling damaged, I maintained a certain sense of self-worth based on my academic success. My academic success served as a counterbalance and served as a salient voice that reminded me that I might have been weak and damaged physically, yet, I was strong intellectually.

As an impoverished child, my self-concept and identity suffered because I honestly did see myself as damaged. I would be an adult before I would become aware of and come to understand that issues with gross and fine motor skills were common among stutterers. It mattered that my brothers criticized me at home and others criticized me at school for not being a good athlete, especially during adolescence. My greatest desire was the same as that of any child, to be accepted and to fit in. Yet, I found myself being a square peg attempting to fit into a round hole. A life lesson learned was that many of the things that appear to be a matter of life and death when we are young often have little to no impact on our success and happiness as adults. I went on to run track during my junior and senior year in high school and was a member of the high school marching band as well. As an adult who later coached successful Y Club basketball teams and played in the Georgia Southern Concert Band, I learned that my not being a good athlete in my teen years did not matter as an adult.

Daily, our lives cross the paths of children who feel damaged, not perfectly round. Such children are aware that they do not quite measure up. They are acutely conscious of the labels imposed on them by others as well as by themselves early in their lives. Their indifference, perceived arrogance, defiant attitude, and tougher than nails image often belie their feelings of inadequacy, their soul is damaged. Middle school children, transecents, are the age group that are most impacted by self-image issues and identity issues. They by nature experience clumsiness; physically, emotionally, and socially as they discover who and what they are to be.

Social perception is the study of how people form impressions of and make inferences about other people. The prevailing message is that in order to fit, one must be perfect, must be perceived as perfect. The damaged goods that my parents bought while being different in outward appearance were of the same quality as those on the grocery store shelves. Their difference in value was due to the perception of the buyer. Having visible imperfections, these goods were ascribed a lesser value. The damaged goods syndrome results when others choose to see the person as substandard and of lower value and the person viewed as such self, identifies with those perceptions. I quickly learned that perception is reality for the one that perceives it to be so. In order to escape the damaged goods syndrome, I had to modify my perception of myself. I had to abandon seeing myself as a *victim* and view myself as a *victor!* This paradigm shift was necessary for me to overcome poverty and other life issues. I learned that I must identify and focus on my strengths while acknowledging but not being identified solely by my weaknesses. In order to have an opportunity to be successful, we must come to the realization that people are not perfect, nobody is perfectly round. We must come to realize that in some way, we are all damaged.

We must realize that our worth is inherent in the fact that we are a unique and divine creation. Being so, each of us is worthy of love, respect, and acceptance. We have a role in life that no one else can fill and a void will remain unless we assume our rightful position in life and in our world. If we are to be successful, we must realize that while *life may not deal all of us a full deck of cards or a winning hand,* we are all dealt a hand. We must know that it is our responsibility to play and make the most of the hand that we have been dealt. Success for each of us is not dependent on having the ideal hand of cards around the table. Success for each of us is playing the hand that we are dealt with the best of our ability. We must realize that success is relative. We must measure success by the extent to which we utilize our God- given talents and abilities rather than measure our success based on the strengths and accomplishments of others. We must know that while all are created equal, the reality is that people are born with differing talents, abilities, and intellect. Real success for each of us lies in fully utilizing all of the talents and abilities with which we have been equipped All too often we spend our lives relegating ourselves to sitting in the back seat of the car of opportunity. Each of us must assume our rightful position and take control over our destination and destiny. Our proper place is in the driver's seat. Getting out of the backseat is a choice that requires effort and determination. Yet, getting out of the backseat is necessary if we are going to drive the car and determine our own destiny.

CHAPTER 8

Life in the Backseat

Two roads diverged in a wood, and I—
I took the one less traveled by,
And that has made all the difference.

Robert Frost 1920

Being a child of poverty, everyone in the family had to work in order to provide for the needs of the family. Mama and daddy married four years after her first husband had abandoned her. Daddy had been married twice before and had two sons by his second wife. My paternal grandmother Ada kept his two sons until her death about four years after mama and daddy married. My two brothers then moved in with us, making us a family of 13 children plus my cousin, Charlie Mae, great Aunt Minnie, and Grandma Carrie. Mama had raised my cousin Charlie Mae from the age of eight after her my mother passed. My brother Kenneth was born in 1959, followed by my being born in 1961 and my sister Marie, the baby of the family, being born in 1962. With the birth of

Marie, our family was complete. A total of eighteen people lived
in our house during my early years.

During my early years, Mama worked on the farm right
along with daddy in the fields. She would pick cotton, peas, and
corn. The children worked right along with her. In addition, she
spent many long days in the dead of winter cleaning and
processing turkeys. By my early teen years, the landowner had
stopped raising turkeys and purchased mechanized cotton
pickers and combines for corn harvesting. Mama began
working as a housekeeper for several families in our
community.

Having finished doing some yard work for a neighbor
for whom mama worked, I was about to get into her car to be
taken home. I walked over to mama to tell her goodbye. Mama
had come prepared to stay the entire day, being the
housekeeper. Mama walked along with me toward the car and
spoke quietly to me saying, *"Get in the backseat."* I stared into
mama's eyes, searching for a deeper understanding of the words
that she had uttered. Obediently, I complied with mama's
command and took my seat in the back of the car. Based on
lessons learned growing up, I instinctively obeyed without
question. Many mixed emotions raced through my mind as I sat
riding in the backseat. I slumped down slightly, hoping that no
one that I knew would see me riding home in the backseat of
the car. A sinking feeling began to develop in the pit of my
stomach as I pondered the situation. My mind trailed back to
the life lessons that mama and daddy had taught me.

I was taught to be respectful and obedient toward all
adults. I was also taught that, even though, there were certain
societal expectations and perceptions in regard to being poor
and Black, I was just as good as the next person. Somehow,

now, I questioned whether or not the lessons that I had been taught were true. Was I really just as good as the next person? Did being poor and Black make me less of a person? If I was just as good as the next person, why did I have to ride home in the back seat when the front passenger seat was unoccupied?

I soon arrived at home and walked into the back yard. As I walked around in the back yard, I felt so conflicted. I felt intense anger coupled with shame. I was angry with mama for telling me to ride home in the backseat. I felt a sense of sense of shame as I replayed over and over the image of my riding home in the backseat in my mind. The ride home reinforced feelings of inferiority that I already felt having been born a child of poverty coupled with being born a chronic stutterer.

As I talked with Mama later that night, she clarified her request for me to ride home in the backseat. Mama explained that her rationale for asking me to do so was for my own protection. I reflected on mama's words within the context of the late 1920's era in which she was raised. Although I was only thirteen years old, I was acutely aware of the differences in the relationship that existed between blacks and whites in the late 1920's era when juxtaposed with the 1970's era. I realized that many of those views about class and race still existed in the 1970's where I lived. By telling me to ride home in the backseat, mama was doing what was expected and deemed safe for most of her adult life and what she deemed safe for me then.

Life in the backseat is a substandard state of existence. Too many individuals relegate themselves to a life of mediocrity because they perceive that this is what is expected of them. Quite often people who are dismissed or relegate themselves to backseat living eventually allow backseat living to become a way of life. Just as the great poet, Robert Frost described in his poem, "The Road not Taken", we can choose which road we travel upon. We cannot choose the family that we are born into, but we can choose the family that we become. We cannot choose our name, but we can determine the level of respect held for our name. We can choose to ride in the backseat and ride quite comfortably as long as we are willing to accept the limitations and destination others prescribe and choose for us. We can choose to ride in the backseat just because that is where we have always ridden because it is the only life we know and is safe. We can also choose the road not taken and refuse to relegate ourselves to a life of mediocrity.

Life in the backseat is safe living as the individual is free of worry about critical life decisions. Life in the backseat is an easy life in many respects. Sitting in the backseat, one has no control over the road taken. Having neither control over the path taken nor the final destination, backseat rider is free to blame the driver and front seat rider for the eventual outcome, their final destination. I was taught as a child of poverty that while being poor defined us economically; I could and would play a role in determining the road that my life would take. Riding in the front seat, taking the road not often taken, and helping to determine our destiny is a choice. Life in the front seat represents a life of shared responsibility. While reality dictates that we must recognize that the roads that we travel upon still have many potholes, the condition of the roads has improved. Life in the front seat says that while I may not be driving, I do have input as to the path took, my final destination.

People in the backseat, today often experience anger similar to that which I experienced while riding home in the back seat that day. Much of this anger is displaced, generated by too many people accepting the limitations that they believe life has put upon them. Rather than continuing to be angry with the driver or front seat rider, the person riding in the backseat must make a decision to refuse to continue to ride in the backseat, thus taking their rightful place in life. It is up to each of us to refuse to relegate ourselves to a life of obscure backseat living. Dr. Martin Luther King Jr. eloquently stated, "A man cannot ride your back unless it is bent." We must straighten ourselves up and take the driver's seat and guide our own destiny.

Mama continued to work as housekeeper for the neighbor and several members of her family until she was well into her 60's. When the neighbor for which mama kept house and worked could no longer drive and pick up mama and bring her back home after work, Mama was allowed to drive the car home. This continued until the neighbor died.

When I started teaching school in Jenkins County, I lived in Statesboro Georgia and commuted to Millen for a time. Not wanting to put so many miles on my car, I began to look for a second car to drive to work. I knew that the neighbor's car that mama drove back and forth to work until the neighbor died was not being driven. I made arrangements with one of the sons of the neighbor and subsequently purchased this car. I drove it for a couple of years before letting my older brother sell it for me. It would be many years later before I recognized the significance of my owning and driving the car that I had been compelled by my mother to ride in the backseat in as a child. Whether consciously or subconsciously, I had taken a painful memory and made it a memorable life event. Refusing to continue to ride in the backseat was to be a theme throughout my life.

Daddy continued to work on the land that we sharecropped until the middle to late 1970s. The owner died in 1972 and the property went to his brother, a business owner in

Maryland. After hiring three different people to oversee the
farming operation, the farm was eventually sold. Daddy stopped
sharecropping and farming and began to drive a fertilizer truck
for a local farm supply store. We still lived on the land as if
daddy still worked for the landowner. During my first year at
Georgia Southern, I came home every weekend. One weekend,
I overheard Daddy telling mama that the owner of the farm
supply store where he worked had offered to let the family
move into a house that they owned in town. Having lived in the
country all of her life and on the property where we lived since
the early 1950's Mama did not want to move to town. More
than our family moving to town, I was most concerned about
daddy still thinking in terms of the boss supplying the workers'
housing as was done when he was a sharecropper.

   I knew that daddy's health was in decline and that he
was in constant pain and could barely walk. This was due to a
lifetime of hard work and a back injury. Where would we live
when Daddy could no longer work? I recalled conversations
that mama and I had before about buying the property where
we lived even though she felt that we had more than paid for it
already through their supposed sharecropper arrangement. We
cleared only $800 after settling each year during the early years.
Somehow, the owner never got around to an in-depth
discussion about our buying the property. Daddy was content
with moving to town and did not see himself as having any
other options.

   I decided that it was time for us to take control of our
destiny as far as a place to live was concerned. I asked mama for
the address of the deceased landowner's brother in Maryland. I
wrote him a letter that weekend. I told him that I was writing
on behalf of mama and daddy. I told him how much I
appreciated how supportive he had been of my family. He had

once offered to pay the full tuition for my brother who was Star Student, to go to medical school. I let him know that daddy's health was in decline and we were living on his property because daddy had previously worked for his family. I indicated that when daddy was no longer able to work, our family would have no place to live. I asked him to let us buy the house that we lived in and a little of the land surrounding the house. I further stated that I was doing well at Georgia Southern but was willing to drop out and get a job in order to help daddy and mama pay for the house and land. I thanked him for his time. I received a reply from him about a week later. He encouraged me to remain in school and told me that he would arrange for us to buy the house and land. He flew down a few months later and completed the paperwork necessary for us to purchase the house and land on which my family had lived since the 1950s. Even though the house was destroyed by fire in 1985, we still live on and own the property. As a child of poverty, I learned through struggle that the road not taken could be rough traveling. I learned that not many choose this road because it requires much of the traveler. Yet, I learned though that if one is to succeed in life, one must be committed to conquering life's obstacles rather than allowing life and barriers to surmount them. We must not be content with being a backseat or front seat passenger. We must take our rightful place and own and drive the car/purchase the land, thus determining our own destiny. We must be willing to conquer whether real or imagined, the beasts in our lives rather than be controlled by them.

CHAPTER 9

The Beast

A feeling of fear enveloped me as I walked through the door. I could see the Beast sitting there on the table glaring angrily at me. Its eyes were shiny black and were fixed on me. I hesitated for a moment and considered running away. I knew though that I had been chosen for this task and had to face this Beast. As I inched closer, I could feel the heat coming from its body as it sat there motionless, saying nothing. Its nostrils were tiny slits that covered both the left and right side of its face. Dim red light emanated from its nostrils. The light became brighter as I came closer. As I neared, I could hear a faint growl coming from the belly of the Beast. The Beast had only one ear, which sat on the table separate from but attached to its body.

My protector, whom I trusted and had been by my side for many years, stood to the right of the Beast. He encouraged me to proceed and announced my arrival to the Beast. I remembered again that I had been called and that it was my responsibility and honor to be chosen to conquer the Beast. I slowly put my hands-on the table beside the Beast. I grasped the

Beast's ear in my hand and placed my mouth close to it. For a moment, I was speechless and could hardly breathe. An overwhelming feeling of fear of failure enveloped me. I was tempted to release the Beast's ear from my grasp and run out of the door. Finding inner strength, I finally began to speak into the Beast's ear. The Beast responded by echoing loudly and repeating each word that I spoke.

As a member of the Johnson County High School BETA Cub, I had been chosen to lead the students and faculty in the Pledge of Allegiance over the intercom. I felt somewhat embarrassed after having finished reciting the Pledge, knowing that I had said it too quickly. I tended to speak quickly in order to get my words out before the stuttering and stammering speech pattern took over. Some of the students in my homeroom were still laughing when I returned to class and later told me that the teacher had also laughed. Overall, I felt somewhat of a sense of pride at having been tasked to do what few had been privileged to be asked to do. There were not many students in my school who had high enough GPAs to be invited to become a member of BETA club. Ironically, there was less than twenty minority students in BETA Club at my high school. While I did not do a perfect job, I did the best job that I could. I chose not to allow the fear of failure to dissuade me. I did not let the possibility of ridicule from my classmates stop me. I was cognizant of the fact that I was a known chronic stutterer. I was however defined by more than my speech impediment. I was a Gifted Education and Honor Student and refused to be limited by and defined only by my weakness. In life, we face many beasts as well as encounter various fears. Beasts and fear control us only if we refuse to confront and face them. The lesson I learned, as a child of poverty was that life is filled with obstacles and beasts both real and imagined. I was taught however that I only failed when I failed to try. Failure for me was always an option but refusing to attempt a task and face the Beast was not. Growing up as a child of poverty, I was taught that I could not quit anything that I had begun no matter how hard the job was. Poverty for my family and me was an ever-present concern yet we persisted in life. Through poverty, we learned resilience. Poverty was viewed by our family as a changeable and not a fixed economic condition rather than as a permanent way of living.

CHAPTER 10

Living in Poverty

According to United States Census data, 49.61 percent of the citizens in Johnson County, Georgia were living below the poverty level 1961; the year I was born. Currently, 20.7 percent of the citizens in Johnson County live below the poverty line. This percentage is slightly above the Georgia rate of 18.2 percent and well above the national poverty rate of 15.4 percent. As a young boy, I was reminded many times of the prevalence of poverty during my developmental years. One particular occurrence takes the forefront in my mind. As was often our practice, one day several of my older brothers walked from home to the town, which was approximately five miles. The community in which we lived was and continues to be called Donovan. Prior to the early 60's Donovan was a bustling farm community complete with its own country store. Life in Donovan centered on farming and agriculture. As a result, there were many shotgun houses scattered throughout the community and along each side of the highway. These shotgun houses were usually filled with large families. Landowners were dependent on this ready workforce and made available dilapidated housing to their workers. Laborers were paid a meager wage for what was often a twelve-hour workday. In some instances, when the landowner owned a store, workers would be given a voucher to be redeemed at the landowner's store as well as providing housing in lieu of wages. There were shotgun tenant houses scattered along the road to town.

As my brothers were walking back from town one day, a heavy downpour struck suddenly. They ran up on the porch of one of the neighboring homes in order to get out of the heavy downpour. As they stood on the porch out of the rain, a lady, who happened to be White, opened the door and invited my brothers inside out of the rain. My brothers thanked her for the hospitality and came inside. Inside the house were the woman who asked them in and her two daughters. As my brothers walked into the house, the woman's two teenage daughters greeted them. The woman, looking embarrassingly down at the floor asked the girls loudly, "Whose panties are these on the floor?" One daughter quickly responded, "Not mine because I have mine on." As my brothers recounted the story at home later, it was quite telling to them that the daughter's response confirmed that this family was just as poor as we were. By the daughter's own admission that she only had one pair of underwear, we realized that we were not alone, that poverty knows no color.

What I took away from the story was life changing in so many ways. As a young child reared in poverty, I had innocently assumed that poverty was limited to poor Blacks living in the rural south. I had assumed that people living in what we termed up north lived a life of luxury. I began to realize that all of the White farm laborers that lived near us shared our plight. I also learned that our White neighbors, similarly situated as we, were more apt to show compassion, being impoverished also. This story has continued to resonate with me throughout my life. It reminds me of the interconnectedness of mankind. It reminds me that we are more alike than we are different and that common issues tend to tear down walls of division and bring us closer together.

I was taught as a child born and reared in poverty that I could not help being born poor because I did not pick the family into which I was born. I was taught that while I could not help being born poor, I could avoid being lazy and nasty. The message to me as a child was that I had dignity and worthy as did others and that I was no better or worse than anyone else. This message was qualified however with the belief that if I wanted to succeed, I could not form relationships with others who lacked vision, discipline, motivation, and who did not share my core values and beliefs. I learned that it was much easier to be torn down and reduced to rubble than it was to lift a person out of the rubble. This was especially true if the person was comfortable living in the rubble. I was taught that my current condition, being born in poverty did not have to become my lifetime plight.

In his 1963 work titled "The Culture of Poverty", Oscar Lewis makes a distinction between a "culture of poverty" and impoverishment. Lewis postulates that not all people living in poverty develop a culture of poverty. Lewis describes residents in a culture of poverty as having developed feelings of helplessness, dependency, and alienation that are sustained over time. Feelings of inferiority and personal unworthiness are also described as symptomatic for the impoverished that adopt a culture of poverty. Lewis describes people who embrace a "culture of poverty" as a people whose primary focus is on their own troubles, living conditions, their own neighborhood, and way of living and see their condition as being permanent.

Impoverished people, unlike the poor who adopt a culture of
poverty, although living in poverty, learn to see similarities
between themselves and others similarly situated as they are. As
a result, the impoverished become class conscious and adopt a
more global worldview and develop a vision for hope and
change. My family, while poor, did not adopt a culture of
poverty. I learned many lessons while living in poverty, as a
result.

It was our daily routine to rise at 6:00 each morning.
We rose early during the week so that we would be ready when
the school bus ran. We arose at the same time on Saturdays to
do work on the farm and on Sundays for church. When school
was out, we rose at 6:00 am to work in the fields each day. Even
if there was no particular task that needed to be done, which
was rare, we were never allowed to lie in the bed beyond this
time. During the day, we were not allowed to sit on the bed.
Daddy and mama's philosophy was that only sorry people lie
around inside. Only lazy people sit on the bed.

My family was blended. My mother was married at
seventeen. She began her life as a mother and laborer on the
farm where we still live. When my mother was a twenty-eight-
year-old mother of eight, her then husband abandoned her. The
oldest child, my sister Mary, was eleven years old and the
youngest child, my brother James, was four months old. I recall
her talking later about working in the fields handling fertilizer
and seed corn and cotton seed and planting crops along with
the other male farm hands to provide for her large family. My
Grandmother Carrie had lived with her while she was married
and continued to live with and assist her after her husband left.
My mother recounted an experience recently that she had at the
local Department of Family and Children Services (DFCAS) in
1954, shortly after her husband abandoned her. She had gotten

a ride to town and had taken all eight children with her to apply
for temporary financial assistance as she was having difficulty
providing for her family. The DFCAS case worker was
incredulous in her response to my mother that day. My mother
reported later that the DFACS worker handling her case told
her that all eight of the children could not possibly be hers.
Once mama provided ample evidence that all eight were indeed
her children, the caseworker responded that some of them
could work and denied my mother any assistance. My mother,
in recounting her response to the caseworker, was adamant that
her children would have better opportunities than she was
afforded and that she would not keep them out of school to
work in the fields as the caseworker had suggested.

My mother did not and could not in her day challenge
the decision of the DFACS. She resumed her work in the field
doing the work of a male farm hand. In recounting this
incident, she affirmed what I had always been taught. I was
taught that it was not the job of the government to take care of
people. Instead, it is the responsibility of the family and each
individual to take care of themselves and each other. That day
my mother vowed to never be in a position of dependency.

As an indication of the impact of poverty during those
years, my sister Marie was the only child to be born in the
hospital. She was born in the hospital only because she had
been a breach and both she and my mother had almost died.
My mother had gone into labor on a Tuesday and had gone to
the local doctor in town. She had been examined and sent back
home and told to wait. She was finally taken to the hospital in
nearby Sandersville five days later upon the recommendation of
the midwife, Ms. Ethel Gonder. The doctor indicated that if she
had arrived at the hospital a few hours later, both mother and
child would have died. Because of her difficult birth, my sister's

shoulder remained discolored and bruised even after she came home from the hospital. As I listened as my mother recounted the events of my sister's birth, I was reminded of the fact that quality and prompt health care was beyond the reach of those living in poverty. Preventive health care was beyond our grasp as well. I did not go to the dentist until I developed a toothache and the tooth had to be extracted. I was a 32-year-old high school principal when I had my first cavity filled.

I have always admired and continue to admire mama's quiet strength. She was strong during an abusive relationship. She was strong after being abandoned with eight children and looked down upon by others including family because she had so many children. She was strong when being denied any assistance to help care for her children. She was strong when she did the work of a male field hand, handling large bags of fertilizer and loading bags of seed corn in the hopper during planting season. She further demonstrated her strength on two separate occasions by her having picked one hundred plus pounds of cotton that day and then having delivered a child that night with only the support of a midwife.

Mama emphasized the importance of being poor but clean by her insisting that even though we were wearing the same clothing to school at least twice a week, clothing had to be washed weekly and starched and ironed before they were worn. She insisted that the boys learn to wash clothing and iron just as the girls did. Keeping the clothes clean for so many was not an easy task. In my early years, I remember mama making lye soap out of potash and pork fat. We had three 18-gallon cast iron wash pots that we used to wash clothes. Our only outside water source then was a faucet at the back door of the house. The only inside water source came from a faucet attached to the water line at the back door and run through a hole in the back wall of the house. Inside the house in this kitchen area, a ceramic-coated metal dishpan sat in a cabinet below the faucet. We did not have a sink anywhere in the house. We would fill galvanized steel buckets that we called foot tubs with water. Foot tubs held five gallons of water. We would carry water from the outside faucet at the back door until each wash pot was filled. A fire would then be made around two of the pots. One pot was for white clothes and linen. The other pot was for colored clothing. The third pot was filled with cold water and served as the rinse pot. A large stir stick made from a tree limb was used to stir the clothes as they boiled as well as to remove them from the boiling water and drop them into the rinse water. After stirring and rinsing laundry in the rinse pot, we would each take a small piece of clothing and wring it out and hang it on the clothesline in the backyard to dry. For larger items, one child would get on each end of the piece of laundry and begin twisting each end in opposite directions until most of the water was wrung out. We would then hang the larger clothing items on the clothesline together. We learned quickly and early the necessity of teamwork and the division of labor through mama's insistence on cleanliness.

This insistence on cleanliness extended into the area of personal hygiene as well. I was 12 years old before we had an inside bathroom and a kitchen sink. By this time, only the youngest three children were still at home plus my niece, Kwan that we raised as if she was a baby sister. During the wash pot clothes-washing era, we had no bathroom. We took a bath at night in a 20- gallon galvanized steel tub similar to the foot tub that we used to haul water to wash clothes in. We termed the larger 20-gallon tub as a washtub. During cold weather, we would heat water with the wood heater that served as our primary heat source in foot tubs and fill the washtub with boiling and cold water until it was just the right temperature.

We took turns going into one of the cold unheated bedrooms and taking a bath each night. We would get up in the morning after someone had made a fire in the wood heater and heat up enough water to "wipe off." "Wiping off "meant washing your face and under your arms and then putting on deodorant before brushing our teeth. During warm weather, we would fill the washtubs with water and lean them up against the front of the house facing the sun. By nightfall and bath time, we would have a washtub filled with water in which to bathe that was just at the right temperature. We did not have an outside toilet at this time. We had an outhouse that was built 50 or more feet away from the house. Being a family in poverty, we could not afford to buy toilet tissue. Instead, we would use old newspaper. We would take sheets of newspaper and rub them together in our hands until the paper was soft and suitable for use. We saved gallon syrup cans and under each bed for use as well. I dreaded having to go to the outhouse at night. I would have to get a piece of fat lighter wood which we used to start fires. I would have to burn it and use it to light the way to the outhouse. Being reared in poverty taught me to think outside of the box in order to find other means to meet our basic needs. In addition, I learned to use what I had at hand and to see the value and utilization of things that others saw as refuse.

Daddy's insistence on cleanliness extended to maintaining the cleanliness of the outhouse. My brother and I dreaded the early part of each summer once school was out because we knew that daddy was going to tell us that it was time to clean out the outhouse. Daddy would make us dig a deep hole a few feet away from the back of the outhouse. He would give us two long shovels and have us scoop any waste that had not decayed and throw it into the hole. This process continued until the back of the outhouse was clean. We would then cover up the removed waste. While daddy was stressing the message of cleanliness and good hygiene, I learned some life lessons. The annual cleaning of the outhouse taught me "if you stir mess, it will stink". I also learned the lesson that if you "play in or hang around mess, you will get mess all over you". Finally, I learned that while some mess decays and goes away, some mess will remain until you make a conscious effort to move it out of your life. I learned from poverty the importance of cleanliness of body, heart, and character. I learned that hanging around bad intentioned people and adverse situations would soil my character, my good name, and reputation. Ultimately I learned that it takes action on our part to remove the undesirable things from our lives and that we cannot just simply wish them away. These experiences in poverty formed the foundation that would shape my thoughts, life, and future. In retrospect, while I lived in abject economic poverty, other aspects of my life were very generous and necessary in order to mold me into what I was to be. I learned to value the family name and wear it well.

CHAPTER 11

"Diddy Waah"

Growing up, I was called Diddy Waah by my father. In poverty-stricken communities and in the Black community, in particular, everyone in the family had a nickname. Nicknames served as a term of endearment. Grandmother Carrie's nickname for me was "boy" and daddy nicknamed me "diddy waah." The nickname came from a popular 1960's song by the American Soul Group, the Adlibs. The song, ""The Boy from New York City"", peaked at No. 8 on the Billboard Hot 100 in 1965. The significance of the nickname "diddy waah" can be found in a particular portion of the song lyrics, which read, "Ooh wah, ooh wah cool, cool kitty. Tell us about the boy from New York City, He's really down and he's no clown. He has the finest penthouse I've ever seen in town. And he's cute in his mohair suit and he keeps his pockets full of spending loot. Ooh whee, say you ought to come and see His dueling scar and brand new car. Ooh wah, ooh wah cool, cool kitty. Tell us about the boy from New York City. Ooh wah, ooh wah c'mon kitty tell us about the boy from New York City."

Although I was born in abject poverty, early on, it was clear to daddy that I aspired to have a better life, as well as the better things in life. The gist of many family conversations centered around the fact that wearing clothes given to us by neighbors and possessing only the bare essentials of life failed to diminish my desire for the trappings that success bring. Each time daddy called me by my nickname; I was reminded that I was not content with life as I then lived. "Diddy Waah" was given to me as a term of endearment laced with a bit of sarcasm. Being called "Diddy Waah" could have moved me to readjust my view and vision to coincide with my impoverished conditions each time my name was called. Rather than accept my aspirations as unreasonable and relegate myself to continuing a cycle of family poverty, when I was called "Diddy Waah, I saw the name as affirming my future.

I was motivated by the stories that I heard and read about people who did much with little simply because they dreamed big. The story of the life of Dr. Mary McLeod Bethune gave me hope. Dr. Mary McLeod Bethune opened the Dayton Educational and Industrial Training School for Negro Girls in 1904 with $1.50, faith in God and five little girls for students. This Training School would later become what Bethune-Cookman University is. Bethune-Cookman, a premier Historically Black College, and University, has graduated more than 13,200 students since 1943.

As a child of poverty, I learned the value and importance of dreams. I as a child of poverty was educated in both segregated and integrated schools. I attended school at Dock Kemp, the integrated K-12 school from 1st to 3rd grade. I attended integrated schools in Johnson County from 4th to 12th grade. Dock Kemp was a culturally rich environment in which the focus was on developing the whole child. I flourished during my early years at Dock Kemp that anything was possible. I learned that the level of success in life could ultimately only be hindered by the girth of our dreams and our refusing to abandon our dreams. I was reminded quite often during my formative years at Dock Kemp School of a poem by Langston Hughes titled, "A Dream Deferred." I became more and more determined to refuse to have my dreams deferred and become enveloped in bitterness and defeat.

There were other significant individuals whose name and legacy helped me to continue dreaming and shaped the direction of my life. One such person was Dr. Benjamin E. Mays. Dr. Mays coined a favorite quote and life verse of mine. He states, "It must be borne in mind that the tragedy of life doesn't lie in not reaching your goal. The tragedy lies in having no goal to reach. It isn't a calamity to die with dreams unfulfilled, but it is a calamity not to dream. It is not a disaster to be unable to capture your ideal, but it is a disaster to have no ideal to capture. It is not a disgrace not to reach the stars, but it is a disgrace to have no stars to reach for. Not failure, but low aim is sin."

Dr. Mays, an American black minister, educator, sociologist, social activist, and the president of Morehouse College in Atlanta, Georgia from 1949 to 1967 is recognized as the architect of Morehouse's international reputation for excellence in scholarship, leadership, and service. The Morehouse School of Medicine evolved from the spirit of excellence, leadership, and service espoused by President Mays. It was established in 1975 with a focus on training primary care practitioners as an offshoot of Morehouse . Morehouse School of Medicine recognized the drastically decreasing numbers of primary care physicians who shunned higher paying specialties and focus instead on the need for urban medicine with a commitment to underserved, usually impoverished populations and its adverse effect on low-income areas. The dream as well as focus of Morehouse School of Medicine was and continues to be to train primary care physicians A recent study by researchers at George Washington University and published in the Annals of Internal Medicine found that graduates of the Morehouse School of Medicine led the list of medical schools whose graduates are most likely to devote themselves to primary care and serving underserved communities.

Dr. Mays dreamed big and cultivated a spirit of scholarship, excellence, and service in all with whom he came in contact. Morehouse College stands today as dream realized rather than a dream deferred. My maternal grandmother, Carrie Lillie Sams and my mother, Carrie Lee sought to instill the power to dream and hope in me growing up. I remember them saying to keep hope because the bottom rail was coming to the top. It would be many years later before I realized the significance of these words. They were loosely quoting the quote, "Bottom rail on top dis time." The quote "Bottom rail on top dis time" is attributed to a Black Union soldier, who in 1865, was guarding a group of Confederate prisoners. The soldier noticed his former master among the group of prisoners. The solider was recorded as having said "Hello massa, bottom rail on top dis time!" My great grandmother, having been born in slavery, instilled in my mother that which was passed down to us that there was always hope for change. Because significant others in my life dared to dream and saw dreams fulfilled, I continued to be proud to be called "Diddy Waah and dared to dream.

CHAPTER 12

The Power of Words in Poverty

*Think twice before you speak, because your words and influence
will plant the seed of either success or failure in the mind of another.*
Napoleon Hill

I remember an event during my sophomore year vividly. It
was a warm spring day in 1977. The sun shone brightly and
my countenance mirrored the weather. As I was headed to
my next class, several students who were in the same grade but
not in the "top group" with me, ran up to me bubbling with
excitement to tell me what had just been said to me in English
class. My brother, Kenneth, a senior, had been recently named
Star Student. This was a significant accomplishment and source
of pride as my brother would be the first Black student at our
school to earn the distinction of being named Star Student since
our school integrated in 1970.

The students had been discussing with our English
teacher the news that my brother had been recently named Star
Student. My brother, Kenneth, myself, and my sister Marie were
known to be good students. My brother Kenneth and I had
both qualified and admitted to the Gifted Education Program.

Students in our school were grouped by ability and those few Black students who were in the "top group were sometimes looked down on by our classmates who were not in the "top group."

My classmates happily reported that in a teacher-led discussion in English class my brother's recent accomplishment of being named Star Student had ensued. Apparently, another student had asked the teacher if she thought that I might be Star Student one day. My classmates reported that the teacher stated, "Kenneth is smart but Hayward is a little wine headed." I showed no visible response to what had been reported and my classmates walked away still laughing. Inside, my feelings vacillated between feelings of embarrassment, anger, and betrayal.

As an adolescent, as is typical of adolescents, acceptance by my peers was imperative to me. I was accustomed to being regularly teased due to my being a chronic stutter and the related issues. Had a student made the comment, I would have brushed it off as I often did. I hid my true feelings from my classmates but deep inside I was angry. I was angry because I was embarrassed by what had been said. I also felt betrayed. I felt betrayed because a teacher as opposed to a fellow classmate, had made the comment. My teachers had always been a source of hope and encouragement as I excelled academically but struggled emotionally and sometimes socially. Sadly, the words of my teacher affirmed how I already viewed myself, not quite as good as my brother, and others. My teacher being an authority figure for me gave more validity to negative comments made about me.

I quickly made an emotional adjustment and acted as if this event had never happened. When I went to the teacher's class later that day, I acted as if I was not aware of what she had said. When I looked attentively at my teacher, I still saw her as a person of authority and intellect. I however no longer respected her as a person. I did as I was taught, "If you cannot respect the person, respect the position." I never reported the incident to the principal or my parents nor did I discuss it with anyone else. During that time, the words of teachers and adults were not questioned. My mother became aware of the incident about five years ago as I recounted the incident at church. In my effort to remind the attendees to refuse to allow people's unkind thoughts and words destroy them or their dreams; I used the incident as an example.

As I ended my recounting of the event five years ago, I proclaimed, "Were she still teaching, I now as superintendent of schools, would be her boss." I could have easily accepted as fact the teacher's comments about me. Instead, I chose to let her words be a motivation to prove her wrong. As a child of poverty, I learned that words are powerful. I learned to keep quiet if I could not say anything to uplift or encourage. Having faced this incident as a child would help me to develop a thick skin and level of self-confidence that persisted no matter the situation.

During the summer of 1987 after being named principal of the Jenkins County Primary School, I attended my last Georgia Vocational Association Regional Meeting. A colleague from another district greeted me and began to talk about my recent promotion to principal. I had expected words of affirmation and support but instead was met with words that could have discouraged me had I allowed them to. In discussing my promotion to principal, this colleague, who was also Black did not congratulate me. Instead, she said, "You must have known how to smile right!" I smiled and did not show the disappointment that I felt in my heart on my face. I took her comment to mean that the highly unusual trajectory that my career had taken in a short time occurred because I knew how to play the game as the slaves did during slavery as evidenced by them making fun of themselves or dancing a jig to entertain the master. The obvious fact that I had been a student-centered and engaging teacher, club sponsor, and coach who went beyond what was expected and done by most was entirely ignored. Being accustomed to negative comments, I chose not to be affected by the observations. The lesson that I learned in poverty about the power of words was not to look for affirmation from everyone. I learned that when you succeed against the perceived odds, you leave people with three options; 1) They can ignore your progress and success 2) They can minimize and discount your success 3) They can be empowered and motivated by your success and move toward greater success for themselves. Through poverty, I learned to silence the voices that did not help to build me up but rather were destructive.

CHAPTER 13

The Meaning and Value of Life

"Life is just a minute only sixty seconds in it, forced upon you, can't refuse it. Didn't seek it, didn't choose it, but It's up to you to use it. You must suffer if you lose it, give an account if you abuse it, just a tiny little minute, but eternity is in it." — Dr. Benjamin E. Mays

We must come to realize that true success is not found in personal gain but in utilizing the talents and resources that we possess for the benefit of others and our world. In my case, there were significant others in my life, who along with my mama and daddy, refused to excuse me from being my best simply because I had a speech impediment and was born into a poor family. While my parents attended to my basic needs, my grandmother was instrumental in making me feel special as a younger child. Grandma Carrie exemplified the unconditional love and acceptance that I needed and desired. Due to eighteen people living in our house I slept in the same bed with Grandma Carrie until some of my older brothers moved to Florida looking for a better life. I was grandma's boy and she made me feel special and loved. Grandma Carrie was somewhat of a recluse and avoided most social settings. She was always content to stay at home as long as I was going to be home. To her, I was always special. To Grandma Carrie; I was always "Boy."

I was taught that while I could not pick my family, I could pick my friends and thereby play a role in determining my destiny in life based on hard work, honesty, integrity, and determination. I was taught that the crowd was generally going down the wrong road and that I must be strong in mind, follow the straight and narrow path, and not follow the crowd. I was taught that I would be most like the people with whom I associated since the association brings on assimilation. *I was also taught that while I could not pick my family, I could pick my friends and needed to choose my associates carefully.* I made a special effort to instill the latter message into my son, Joey during his teen years.

I used a publishing program to make a sign with a mirror as the backdrop that said, "Your Friends Are A Reflection Of Your Future And The True You." As is common with teens, he thought that I was too involved in keeping track of with whom he regularly associated. I used this sign to drive home a salient point. "We become more alike those with whom we associate and develop a bond with". Children with structure and consistency often attempt to live out vicariously the life of their alter ego through their friends despite being reared in optimum conditions. When the opportunity presents itself, they adopt the lifestyle of their friends. While it was never my intent to ascribe a greater value or worth to any individual, it was my intent to hammer home a lesson that I learned as a child of poverty. My mother often told us, "You are no better or worse than anybody else, but there are some people that you are above." I learned that if I hung out with persons with no vision, goals, or self-control, I risked becoming more like them. I learned that it is much easier to be pulled down than it is to lift a person up.

I remember that it was an unusually warm winter day, Thursday, December 20, 1984, the day that daddy had been rushed to the hospital. I walked into daddy's room, greeted him, and stood next to his bed. I looked up at the monitor next to his bed. His vital signs were good for someone who just suffered a heart attack at home. Daddy was alert and was expected to be moved out of intensive care on Saturday. Despite it being about 72 degrees outside, there was coolness in the room. I stood there somewhat nervous as I tried to think of words to say. We talked a little, I did most of the talking. I took a long look at daddy lying there. Daddy, a big man who weighed more than three hundred pounds, had a deep, booming voice to match his stature. I had always pictured daddy as being strong and invincible. The man who had always talked very loudly using choppy phrases with that booming voice now lay silent. As a boy, I witnessed him run down an errant stray cow even though he weighed more than 300 pounds. The man that I loved but feared was no longer able to run. Due to hard work and a back injury, he could now barely walk.

As I watched my daddy lying in the bed, I felt this sudden urge to say something to daddy that I had been afraid to say before now. I took a deep breath. I could feel my tongue begin to move quickly in my mouth as I attempted to form the words. Instinctively, being a chronic stutter, I knew that whatever words came out of my mouth either would be halting or rapidly said. Would daddy understand what I said? Would daddy respond in anger? Would daddy respond lovingly? Would daddy respond at all? I stood there speechless for a moment. I finally regained my voice and looked at daddy and for the first time in my life said, "I Love you". Daddy continued to lay there. He was silent. He did not respond.

With the words that I had longed to hear and to say, I walked out of daddy's room. I was disappointed but not surprised that daddy had not responded. After all, I had followed him around from childhood into adulthood learning much from him. I admired his strength and intelligence. Mama previously reminded me that I as a little boy would follow daddy everywhere around the house and say, I've got a pretty daddy." Daddy and I worked closely together on the farm and around the house throughout my childhood and teenage years. Daddy demonstrated his love for me by providing for me. This was the mindset of his generation. Shouldn't that be enough? Did I expect too much by wanting him to say, I love you? Suddenly, I felt happy that I had finally told daddy what I had longed for him to say. I felt proud of myself for being strong. I felt as proud as I had always wanted daddy to be of me.

Daddy was to be moved out of the intensive care unit on Saturday and I had made plans to visit him again. Early that morning as I lay in bed asleep, the phone rang. Mama was on the phone. She told me that the hospital had called and said that Daddy had another heart attack and the family needed to get to the hospital as soon as possible. I quickly jumped up, threw on some clothes, and began my trip back to Sandersville. When I arrived at the ICU waiting room, I saw my baby sister and older brother sitting in the waiting room with mama. I looked at Mama. I was about to ask how daddy was doing. Mama said, "He's gone!" I took a deep breath and held it for what seemed like minutes. Finally, I exhaled.

I had always planned to return home and care for mama and daddy once I was established in my career. I never expected daddy to die before his 55th birthday even though I knew that his siblings and father died younger than 54 years of age. On the day, my daddy died I, even though I was the youngest of daddy's sons, became the man of the family. I decided that day that I would never again wait to say I love you to those that I cared about. Although I told daddy, "I love you" for the first and last time on his death bed, I felt at peace about having said the words that I had so longed to hear for the first time in my life. I vowed that day to sow and show love to all with whom I came in contact. Unlike the song character, Doo Waah Diddy that I was nicknamed after, I was not a boy from New York City. I was raised in poverty in the Deep South. I chose to remain in the rural south where the need is so great. I vowed never to live or work more than an hour's drive by car from my mother. As an educator, I never attained the level of wealth necessary to own a penthouse like the one that Doo Waah Diddy owned. Yet, my life has been rich and enriching. The greatest lessons that I have learned were framed while responding to the oft said statement, "Just look at what you have become!"

CHAPTER 14

Appreciation, Love, Value

The real measure of what we become in life is not based on the titles we carry nor the positions that we hold nor the things we possess. The actual measure of what we become is determined by what we have become in the lives of others. The greatest measure of our success is the extent to which we have used our God-given abilities and skills in giving life and hope to others.

The day that daddy died, I pledged that I would make sure that everyone with whom I encountered felt that were appreciated, valued, and loved. As a teacher, I let my students know that I loved them and wanted the best for them. As I principal, I disciplined with love and dignity. While research depending on the authors view, discourages the use of any type of physical punishment when disciplining students, I did spank children for severe behavioral infractions. I believed in keeping students in the classroom and in school. With the exception of incidents involving a weapon or a severe fight, I did not suspend children from school. When a student was brought in by a teacher for misbehaving, I heard both the teacher's and the student's side. After reading the write-up and listening to each side, I made a decision as to the proper response to this situation. Regardless of the response to the child's choice of behavior, I would always ask the teacher to leave the child with me for a minute. We talked about what poor decisions had been made as well as what the best option or response was. I ended by telling them that I loved them and wanted them to do and be their best. I often hugged them as well.

Times have changed and I would caution educators and care providers to be very careful with regard to physical contact with children today. As Jenkins County Schools Superintendent, it was a common occurrence for my former students, both male and female to walk up to me, greet me, and give me a big hug. I remember a particular event when I attended a basketball game one night. A former student that I had not seen in years, who was now an adult and a father himself, walked over to where I stood on the back wall of the packed old gym. He gave me a big hug and caught me up on recent life events. Later that night, one of the local police officers who we hired to work security at sporting events, told me, "that young man that came up and hugged you, he has been a drug dealer." Having left Jenkins County for five years before returning as superintendent, I had missed out some of the early adult lives of my high school students. My response to the officer was that the student loved and respected me because I had loved and respected him unconditionally as a student. I reiterated that I responded to this student based on what I knew that he could be rather than what others perceived him to be. When we love students enough to push them to improve, excel, and identify them by their strengths rather than weaknesses and their future rather than their past, we can change their lives. Children need positive, healthy relationships with adults where a distinct line is drawn between adult and child. It is not the job of adult care providers to be the child's best friend. It is our job, however, to be each child best example and biggest coach and cheerleader. What I hope that I have become is a beacon of hope for those who feel that they just do not quite measure up. In particular to those living in poverty, I hope that I serve as an example of what hope, faith, determination, and hard work can accomplish. "I was born Black, poor, and handicapped. I am still Black, I am not rich but comfortable. I still stammer every now and then.

CHAPTER 15

Uncle Sam's Plantation

My life has been enriched by my struggles and I am stronger and better because of my struggles. I had no choice in determining my race and gender. I do, however, have a role in determining whether I continue to be identified as poor and damaged. Accomplished author Star Parker best sums up my sentiments about poverty. In her 2003 work, "Uncle Sam's Plantation, Parker often speaks about poverty. Parker, spent years on public assistance, overcame poverty and became a successful business owner; an accomplished author and speaker. Parker believes as I do, that the hope for those living in poverty can be found in a change in attitude based on developing a more optimistic and forward-thinking pattern of thinking.

Hope is found in the hearts of each and every person who makes a conscious decision to leave poverty behind and strive for something greater and better. None of us are perfect and never will be. Some of us may even feel damaged, inferior. We must realize though that it does not ultimately matter about how we look and talk. What matters most is the content of our character and our refusal to relegate ourselves or allow others to assign us to a substandard existence. We as a people, especially families, have an obligation to assist the poor and needy. We can best assist those living in poverty with the opportunity and ability to acquire meaningful work and job skills. Once properly equipped it can be up to each individual to determine his or her destiny. It is not the role of government or others to pull those living in poverty out of the mire. It is the responsibility of each of us to play the hand that we are given and play it to the best of our ability. It is the role of government and others to help remove barriers, self-imposed and otherwise so that people have the opportunity to change their lives. Our world will be a better place because when opportunity knocked, we all answered. *Hayward*

Made in the USA
Charleston, SC
05 April 2015